Contents

FORWARD

On paper, turning eighteen makes you an adult, which is everything that a child wants to be. My second year of University I moved out for real, not into a residence to be governed by my community advisors. I signed my first lease, got my own furniture and kitchen supplies and I finally felt like an adult. My housemates and I decided on a house that was run by a property management company, which felt more personable and safer than an absentee landlord. Not only did they mostly work with student rentals, but they also worked with my mother, who owned properties in the area. We trusted them and we thought they would support us with whatever we may encounter throughout the year. But we were severely mistaken.

From the day our tenancy began as we started moving in, we were greeted with an absolute disaster. We thought being adults would finally mean that people started taking us seriously, but sadly this was not the case. Whenever we brought up an issue, our washing machine not working properly, mold in the bathroom, a warm fridge, a door frozen shut or a flood in the basement, nothing was ever resolved until one of our parents called the property managers and demanded they address the issue.

Second year was one of the most stressful years of my life, constantly dealing with all these issues and trying to get our property managers to take us seriously instead of ignoring us and hoping we would let it slide. We could not have gotten through this without the assistance of my mother Lynn and Tom. At the time Tom owned the property management company we were dealing with but did not know about many of these issues until after our lease had expired. With their help we were able to take the property management company to the Social Justice Tribunal of Ontario and seek compensation for the negligence, including entering our home without notice; and as a house of six girls, we won.

The only reason we knew what they were doing was wrong was because of my mother, who told us it was wrong. Sadly, so many students do not have this luxury and because of this, landlords tend to take advantage of students. If I had access to this guide before I started house hunting in my first year, I would have done so many things differently. We were only looking at the superficial aspects of the house and not deeply into any potential maintenance problems, why would we? As adults, when you buy a home there are house inspectors for that, and it's just one year right? <u>Wrong</u>.

There are so many things that I now know that I wish I had before I signed my lease. School is stressful enough, we shouldn't have dealt with all the problems that we did. If I knew my rights as a tenant, I know circumstances would be different. This guide was created to protect students from being taken advantage of as tenants by properly educating them on their rights and what to look out for. Now you will know all the red flags before signing your lease, so you don't pay extra money for illegal deposits. You will know when to stop and say, "hey, this isn't right" and rectify it before it goes too far. You will know how to be an adult who knows their way around the world of housing, instead of being treated like a child.

Thank you, Tom, for writing this guide for students so they know their legal rights as a tenant, and we can stop these issues from happening. Better late than never.

Liv Weller

A NOTE TO PARENTS

You probably think your work is almost done. Once they finish school they will be out of the house and on their own. This may be a bad time to lay out the statistics regarding the number of over thirty "children" moving back into the family home.

Take the time to read through this guide yourself, in my experience your time is so limited and percentage wise, most parents cannot accompany their children to home viewings. Through my experiences, I hope I have laid out enough groundwork to help them navigate the next few years trouble free and learn a few things along the way.

INTRODUCTION

Throughout this guide I have repeated certain details and with repetition comes understanding which leads to knowledge and improvement. I hope you never have the need for most of it. Your journey in higher learning should be pleasant and memorable. In life there will always be something or someone that lays down directly in front of you, interrupting your journey. There are no accidents, the word itself should be stricken from our lexicon. You are texting and driving, then you rear-ended the car in front of you. Is that an accident? No, you were not paying attention. When you pay attention, then in most cases you can easily step over or around obstacles. The ones that blindside you require knowledge, experience and at times guidance to overcome.

I am a property manager. I have witnessed some of the most deplorable living conditions, landlords and tenants. Imagine for a moment waking up to a foot of raw sewage in your basement. Now imagine it takes the landlord a week to clean it. That happened at a student home. Another landlord allowed his three tenants to reside in his home with three feet of sewage in the basement. That went unattended for over three months. I have also witnessed firsthand a multitude of "scams" designed to separate you from your money and place you in harm's way with properties that are simply put: infested with mold, bugs, rodents are overpriced and dangerous.

This guide is intended to inform and protect you and not a means to market myself or my business. I will never mention my company. My experiences in property management have left me with a desire to exit the profession and perhaps before I do just that, I can leave you with some advice that will assist you during your years living off campus.

Initially, I was going to provide you with a comprehensive list, including full names, addresses and telephone numbers of these "con artists" and slumlords. When I told my lawyer, his head exploded. Not a pretty site. Thankfully, I wasn't wearing white! We live in a litigious world and I have no desire to spend the next few years in Civil Courts defending the truth. All is not lost, there are great landlords out there. This guide will help you gravitate towards them.

"Landlord" refers to the homeowner, their agent or representative, including a property manager, management company, real estate agent or real estate company. Many homeowners use the services of an outside party to maintain their rental property. These parties will generally deal with the tenants, rent collection, tenant disputes, contractors for repairs, city officials and Fire Inspectors. Landlord representatives are equally bound to follow the rule of law and are subject to penalties. If you don't know your rights, the playing field is not level.

Reputable landlords have twenty-four-hour contact numbers for emergencies and the personnel or contractors available for those necessary repairs.

CHAPTER 1

HOUSE HUNTING

It's time. Choose wisely.

Whenever you rush, the probability is high that you will make a mistake. If you are prepared long before the housing rental season begins your odds will vastly improve. Once you sign a lease you will be in that home for at least one year. Your best choice is choosing a property that you can reside in until graduation. Moving a few times over the course of your schooling can be tedious and stressful. Exams are stressful enough. Locking in a home for the duration can also give you negotiation leverage with the landlord. Many landlords pay a tenant placement fee. This fee usually averages seventy-five to one hundred percent of one month's rent, which is significant versus an annual rental increase in the two percent range per year. Negotiate whenever you can. If your group is happy with its accommodations and has decided to stay for the full term, speak to the landlord about perhaps waiving the yearly increase. A landlord's greatest desire is to have a long-term tenant that pays the rent on time, doesn't cause problems or calling because a light bulb burnt out. If you are that type of tenant, then the probability of negotiation is high. Landlords

1

are not interested in whether you have proper credit, they understand that you are students, in most cases, there is no application process, just a lease signing. They may require your parents to co-sign (guarantee) the lease.

STEP 1

Get your group together, generally four to six student groups are ideal. But choose your group wisely. For example, in order to save money, some students double up on rooms. If the owner finds out he can and will raise the rent or demand the unauthorized party leave. This is because you are using more utilities and resources in the home which equates to higher costs. Don't count on a landlord being dumb, you could be living next door to his family, friends or even them. Now the student "couples" that double up in my experience are problematic. Student couples where the companion is or isn't a student. When you have an all-female home and suddenly there is a male companion living in the home you can imagine the level of discomfort for the other female students. I have had instances where parents visit unexpectedly, and it was ugly. This can lead to several students leaving the home and relocating. Whenever you sign a lease as a group, the students that remain in the home are responsible to find new roommates. Imagine trying to do that in the middle of the school year.

The secret is being prepared for and discussing all contingencies with your group. You are adults, friends can become enemies. Get it all on the table beforehand, set the ground rules. If you have only one person in the group that wants to live in a "Frat House" atmosphere, you will quickly run into problems. The most successful groups are usually in the same academic programs. Now if your group is small, the same applies. Talk it out with the students already living in the home or who have rented the remaining rooms. That initial fit makes moving forward much more comfortable. Many rental homes average four to six rooms and the best homes go fast. The nicest, cleanest and closest to campus disappear quickly and it's very important not to waste time during your search. Regardless of your group size, try to get everyone there for the showings.

STEP 2

1. Decide on your budget. What is the absolute highest rent you can afford, individually and as a group? Start there, understanding that the lowest rental fees for properties are generally the poorest quality ones. You

may be in school, but the real world is exactly like off-campus housing. There will be many issues with homes advertised with too good to be true prices.

2. Discuss the maximum distance from campus your group is willing to live. Of course, the further away you are the less expensive the rent will be in most cases. Consider the public transit schedules, access to on-campus resources that may leave you walking a great distance in the early morning hours after research or study sessions on campus.

3. Talk to each other openly and honestly. Of course, there will be students that simply cannot afford opulent accommodations. Some students will chip in a little more to even things out. Your current financial situation is temporary so try not to over extend yourself.

4. At this point have one month's rent ready to electronically transfer to the landlord once you have chosen your home. Try to avoid several individual transfers, put all the funds into one group members account.

STEP 3

1. Book as many showings in one day as possible. I've had hundreds of students in all group sizes and only one or two students per group show up and they're taking pictures. This may certainly lead to you missing out on the best spots because you must go back to your group and consult with them and go over the pictures. This is not the best way to do it, your entire group should be present unless you have the comfort level within the group that one of you can view the home and decide for the group. I strongly recommend that you go as a group and decide together.

2. Gather as much information as possible on the home and the landlord. Never be afraid or embarrassed to ask. A landlord that avoids answers should make you weary.

3. Speak to the students living there if possible. Ask about past or current issues with the home or landlord. Those students are leaving, they have no reason not to be perfectly honest. Of course, try not to ask in front of

the landlord, you will get much more information that way.

4. Individual room door locks should never be padlocks. Aside from the hilarity that has ensued in the past as a result of roommates locking each other in their rooms, forcing each other to crawl out windows, it's dangerous in an emergency.

BASEMENT ROOMS

Basement rooms are almost always cheaper to rent but watch out for the following;

1. A room without a window is not a bedroom.
2. Basement bedrooms must have an escape window. See figure EW1.

Figure EW 1

3. A fire on the main floor or in the basement can trap you in your room. An escape window has a latch mechanism that allows the entire window to open inwards, remain open and allows you room to escape through it. Think twice before choosing to rent in a basement with non-compliant windows.

4. Does the stairway exit the home directly or does it lead to the center of the home requiring you to navigate the main level to find an exit in the event of a fire?

5. Is the basement damp or cold? This is a sign that water is leaking into the basement. If you see dehumidifiers, avoid renting. Many times, there will be one dehumidifier in each room as well as in the common area. If you see this pass. Dampness leads to mold. You cannot always see mold. Forced air heating systems circulate poor quality air throughout the entire home leading to respiratory issues. Also, do you have to drain the units? In the frenzy of showings, you may not realize how loud a dehumidifier can be. Good luck sleeping. Are the forced air furnace and gas water heaters in separate enclosed rooms? These units can also be very loud.

6. Do you see Carbon Monoxide (CO) and smoke detectors? Basements usually have low ceilings and CO and smoke will rapidly envelop the basement.

7. Ask the landlord if they have installed a backflow prevent-or valve. This device protects the basement from raw sewage backing up into the basement.

STEP 4

Now that you have decided

Pick your top three or four homes. The name of the game is first come first serve. The application process, if any, is simply a formality. You will find landlords ready to accept a deposit before you walk out the door during a showing. This stage is "dog eat dog". Take note, if you see landlords accepting multiple deposits or asking for two months' rent as a deposit be careful! You may find yourself in con man town. Even in the most desperate circumstances never send money online by Western Union etc., for a home you did not view yourself. Be wary of completely empty homes. Ask the landlord for photo identification and take a picture of it and their vehicle license plate. Never feel embarrassed to ask a landlord for identification. Once your satisfied send your one-month deposit electronically.

Be sure to include in the note section of the transfer the following;

- "Rental deposit for"
- Full Address of the home
- "Rental deposit to"
- Your full name(s)
- Your contact information

Electronic payment provides you with a detailed digital receipt that includes the landlord's information. Use this method monthly should you decide to pay this way moving forward.

Generally, the landlord will request post-dated cheques to cover the remainder of the rental term. Basically ten (10) post-dated cheques. In many jurisdictions, the law does not require you to pay rent this way. I will say it makes everyone's life easier. You can also pay your monthly rent as follows:

a. Electronic funds transfers

b. Pre-Authorized payments directly from your account to the landlords. You will need a void check from the landlord to set this up with your bank.

c. Pre-Authorized debit payments are also arranged through your bank.

d. Cash of course, but not recommended.

Be prepared with the second rental payment a day or two before the first of the month.

Only after:

1. You check the lease for the "bed bug clause". It may be included and holds you responsible for treatment which can cost thousands of dollars.

2. You have all reviewed the lease, accepted and signed it.

3. You check the dates on the lease. Confirm your move-in date and time.

4. On the lease or in a separate handout the landlord should have included all contact information including twenty-four-hour emergency number(s).

5. Confirm the section of the lease that details utilities. Do you pay or does the landlord? If you are responsible for the utilities do you have to call the utility companies to put them in your name? If you are paying rent plus utilities but are not required by the landlord to transfer

them to your name do not pay them unless you are supplied with the bills in the landlords' name with the address of your house.

6. Confirm the full address of your new home is on the lease.

7. Check that the Landlord signed the lease.

8. Confirm what appliances, common or bedroom furniture is included with the home.

9. Confirm that all exterior door locks, garage, and shed locks have been changed. Generally, individual room doors are not but should be.

10. Expect that no other monies are requested at that time. There are some jurisdictions were key deposits are legal, but this guide would be as big as a phone book if I included the list. While you are quickly searching online for "Are key deposits legal?" in your jurisdiction you probably will need to also search "What is a phone book?" LOL

11. At that time expect the keys. One full set for each member of your group, not one set and "you go copy them yourselves". All the students must be provided with keys at the lease signing.

12. Do not label key tags or keys with your home address.

STEP 5

Move out/Move in day

Open a dialogue with the current students in your new home if possible, find out what time they will be moved out. Although the landlord advised you during the lease signing, it may be a good idea to double check. Sometimes things do not go as planned. Be patient that day as there might be delays.

- Moving trucks get double booked (so book early) or they break down.
- Friends or family may not make it.
- Poor weather conditions are possible.
- If you ordered furniture it too may be delayed.

Remember also that if you are moving your possessions into your room, always lock the door. There will be many people traveling in and out of the home.

CHAPTER 2

SCAMMERS, SCAMS, SKETCHY AND SHADY!

Trust your instincts. If something does not feel right, chances are it is not.

They are out there. They do not care if you are a student. After all, your money is a good as anyone's.

THE RENT IS TOO GOOD TO BE TRUE SCAM

"There are so many people texting me, it won't last. First come first serve. I will hold it for you guaranteed if I get a deposit."

Online ads for rentals asking for deposits without you seeing the home. Sounds crazy, right? It happens. Especially close to the end of the rental season. Desperation can make fools of us all. Never turn over a deposit for a property you have not physically seen and remember avoiding cash, so you have a digital trail.

CONGRATULATIONS, YOU AND THIRTY OTHERS JUST RENTED THE SAME HOUSE

Viewing homes that are completely empty, no furniture or tenants? Be wary, a scammer knows the owners are away, breaks into the home, or poses as an agent to get the key lock box code. They post the ads, some even put out for rent signs and usually, the rental price is great. The scammer arranges multiple showings and collects all the deposits. On moving day there could be thirty of you parked outside. They will even ask for first and last because they have a good feeling about you and are certain the owner will approve.

THE UTILITY SCAM

You rented the property and utilities are extra. All is good. Then the landlord shows up with handwritten pages of what each student owes for the utilities. The alarm bells should be going off now. Never hand over money unless you see and retain a copy of the actual utility bill. The address on the bill must match your address. Others have offered discounts on the bill(s) if everyone pays cash. That may be a sign that the hand-written bills are inflated by up to twenty percent or more. If the landlord refuses to give you an actual copy of the bill(s) then if it looks and smells fishy, its fishy. Keep money aside for the utilities and wait for the landlord to file with the Tribunal or the courts against you. At that point, they can explain the scam to the Judge. They will use this tactic in hopes of intimidating you. They will threaten the disconnection of services. Illegal, illegal and oh yes illegal.

THE MEMBERSHIP CAPER

During the lease signing, you are asked to join a club for let us say one hundred dollars. This "exclusive club" keeps you updated on campus events and blah blah. At the end of your tenancy, it is refundable once you hand in your house keys. Do I have to say it? Key deposit. Let the university keep you up to date on events. Most students forget about the club and the deposit. Never feel intimidated to join any so-called club.

THE RENOVATION HIEST

"Oh yes, these renovations will be completed before you move in" Do you have any idea how difficult it is to get a contractor to finish a project on time? Be wary of homes undergoing extensive renovations. You may have heard that the landlord must put you in a hotel until the home is ready. What if he doesn't? Of course, you can sue. Where are you living while your suing?

THE SKETCHY PEST CONTROL GUY

Treatment has been arranged at your home. Whether your responsible for payment or the Landlord, its beneficial to ensure that the work is completed as promised. If gel treatment for roaches or traps are being used, you can remain in the home. If chemicals or powders are utilized, then you need to be away from the home for up to eight hours after treatment is complete. I have personally caught a pest control technician leaving the home after fifteen minutes for a bed bug treatment. This is nowhere near the time required. Then a bill was received for nearly nine-hundred dollars, that was for the first treatment. Hang around outside the home and inform the technician that if they need anything your just outside.

CHAPTER 3

YOUR RIGHTS

Throughout North America Landlord and Tenant laws may vary but are generally the same.

They are created in part to protect the rights of tenants but should never be abused. I have no mercy for slumlords but taking advantage on both sides creates an atmosphere that will cause your tenancy to become fraught with problems. If you have exhausted all methods of communication with the landlord, never hold back your rent. If your rights are being violated make your way to the Tribunal and depending on where you live, the local court and deposit the rent with them once you have filed your complaint. In most cases, there is a filing fee, but you can recover those costs once your case is successful. I recommend buying a notebook and leaving it in the common area. Whenever there are property issues any of the students can enter it in the book with the date and time, including conversations with the landlord or their maintenance personnel. I can't stress enough how valuable this can be later, especially in court. Print every email or text and staple it in the book. If you need to go to court, you will have to provide hard copies of all your digital evidence. Once you are notified of your hearing date you can explain your case. The moment the court sees you are paying rent to them, they know they are dealing with a competent and responsible person. I can't tell you the number of cases where it was obvious the landlord was a real $#!+, and the tenants showed up with evidence binders that would put some lawyers to shame. The Judge could not hear the tenant's evidence, not a single word, because the landlord filed an application for eviction for non-payment of rent. In court, rent is rent. I cannot emphasize recordkeeping enough.

a. You have the right to exclusive possession of the property you have rented. If the home has a garage, storage shed or driveway, be sure that they are included in your lease. This will help eliminate the nightmare of having the owner or their associates circumvent exclusive possession by accessing these outbuildings. It is used as an excuse by some to keep an eye on the property whenever they wish. Even so, notification is required to be on the property.

b. The landlord or any repair person must have provided you with twenty-four-hour notice prior to attending your property. If you have not received proper notice you can refuse entry.

c. If anyone attends your property without your prior consent call 911. This includes the landlord.

d. Please do not call 911 on the gas, electrical or water meter technicians.... not cool. They will walk onto your property with a hand-held meter to read the device from the exterior of the house. They are usually there for thirty seconds.

e. In the event of an emergency, both property or medical, the notice period is waived. This means that under those circumstances the landlord, Police, Fire and EMT services do not have to provide notice.

f. You have the right to quiet and continued enjoyment of your property. In other words, the landlord or anyone associated with them can't harass, coerce or bother you. Please note the landlord equally has those rights.

g. You have the right to live in a dwelling that is in a good state of repair, that is fit for habitation. Even if you knew there were issues when you signed the lease it does not mean that you accept those issues. Some landlords will include an "as is" clause in the lease. THIS IS NOT LEGAL.

h. You or the Landlord cannot change the locks.

i. You are responsible for the costs of any repairs due to your neglect.

There have been many instances where miscommunication or lack of, have caused issues between the landlord and tenants. It is important to understand that in this case its best to realize that from the moment you contact the landlord, they or their contractors may arrive in as little as thirty minutes. Regardless of past issues with your landlord, I recommend not refusing entry and allowing the work to be done. Remember in any emergency the owner can exercise the right to enter without notice to prevent further damage to persons or property.

CHAPTER 4

24 HOUR EMERGENCIES

This chapter deals with the landlord's responsibilities regarding response times for various issues with your home. This is a perfect opportunity to write down your local fire inspector and property standards telephone numbers and post them in the common area of your home or the notebook.

Unfortunately, there are landlords that do not follow the rule of law or even decency. Prior to signing a lease ask about twenty-four-hour service telephone numbers and policies.

There are specific circumstances that require a landlord to act within twenty-four hours.

24 HOUR RESPONSE LIST

SMOKE & CARBON MONOXIDE DETECTORS

Remember to test weekly by pressing the test button. Should any of these devices fail they must be replaced within twenty-four hours. No exceptions. Otherwise, contact your local fire inspector. In many areas, the inspector will provide a detector if the landlord fails to abide by the order to comply and they will fine the landlord.

1. ANY DOOR OR EXTERIOR WINDOW

Front, back, side and upper levels that cannot close and lock or that has a broken window large enough for someone to access or unlock the door must be repaired or replaced immediately. Any situation that would permit an intruder to access the home is to be treated as an emergency. Now keep in mind that such after hour services are costly and the landlord may choose to provide a temporary solution, such as boarding up a window. This is acceptable on a short-term basis to provide security.

2. WATER

Every residence must have a constant supply of hot and cold running water, primarily for sanitation purposes.

If you don't have hot water, under no circumstances do you try to re-light the furnace, on-demand water unit or boiler. Even if you think you know what you are doing, serious injury or death may result. Boil water while you are waiting for the repair(s). Its inconvenient, but so are skin grafts.

If the landlord fails to communicate with you and provide a timeline for the repair(s), call your local property standards office. In most cases, they will arrange for a licensed technician to make the necessary repairs and bill the owner. You are never required to pay for any water supply repairs.

3. REFRIGERATORS & STOVES

Most student homes have multiple refrigerators and stoves. If they break down, they are usually replaced with a used model and not repaired. A refrigerator can hold temperature for up to forty-eight hours if the door is kept closed. Every time you open the door you will shorten that exponentially. If possible, relocate your items to another refrigerator. Although this is considered an emergency expect a replacement within two to three days.

Appliances such as microwaves, dishwashers, kettles and coffee makers are to be maintained by the landlord (if provided). Expect secondary appliances to require a little more time to replace or repair.

ROOF/WALLS

After any major rainfall, you may notice leaks. The drips requiring buckets are a nuisance but note that water is a strange substance. Just because water has found its way into your home does not mean that the damage is directly above the leak. Keep in mind that it may take a few days to find the issue on the roof or source a leaking pipe. Once it has been identified, then repairs can be made quickly.

Major leaks or collapses must be dealt with immediately. You can expect the roofing company to be on site and temporarily tarp the roof area and then return to effect repairs once the rain has stopped. If a major leak stems from a damaged water pipe, immediately shut off the main water valve at the meter and contact the landlord.

CHAPTER 5

FIRE SAFETY

Most home fires are often from cooking, electrical malfunction, space heaters, fireplaces, and smoking. Despite popular belief, fire is not what kills you...smoke does.

If you are fortunate enough to wake up before you succumb to smoke inhalation your eyes and airways will be filling with smoke. They will burn, you will panic. You might remember to drop down low to the floor. Your crawling around, lungs and eyes burning, trying to escape, literally blind, crying out if you can to your roommates to warn them or for help. Thinking if you can just get to the hallway so you can do just that. Did you remember to check the door to feel if it's hot? You just burned your hand trying to open the door, panic heightens, you lose consciousness, you didn't make it.

The safest and fastest way out was about six feet away or closer, your bedroom window. You were panicked, frightened and confused. You were not the first, and unfortunately not the last.

Smoke will fill a house at light speed. It will occupy every square inch of space including your lungs, it will feel like the fire itself is inside you and render your eyes useless. Couple this with panic and you can understand that the odds are stacked heavily against you. Lack of, or faulty smoke detectors (this includes detectors found without batteries) have been a major determining factor in fire-related fatalities. This is, simply put, stupid. This is your life. You're at your most vulnerable while you sleep, and a smoke detector keeps silent watch twenty-four hours a day. Here are some tips:

Prepare a Fire Escape Plan with your roommates. Practice it.

- Close your eyes.
- Get out of bed.
- Alert your roommates by yelling fire.
- DO NOT look for your phone. You will need both hands free. #dead
- DO NOT try and get dressed.
- Find your window.
- Remember the window screen is easy to punch or push out. Do not fumble around in an emergency looking for the release tabs, Knock it out.
- Know exactly how to unlock and open your window.
- Have a small step stool in front of your window if you require it to exit. Figure EW1
- Run to your neighbors, call 911.

This little exercise may just save your life. Practice it.

SMOKE DETECTORS

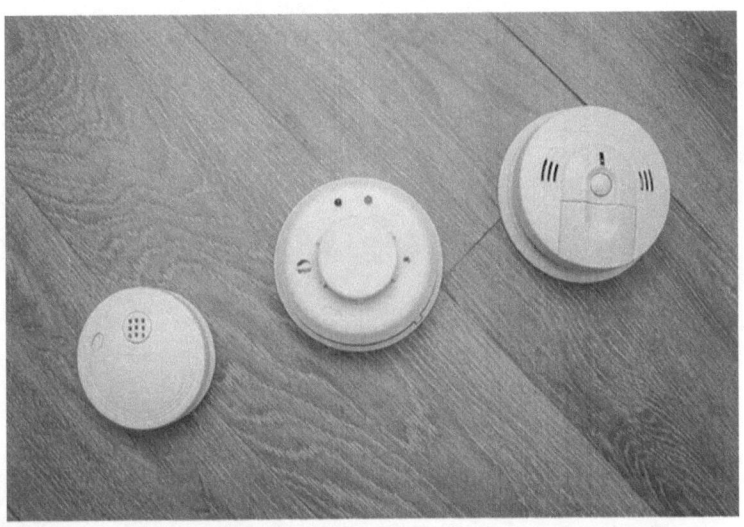

Smoke detects must be located on every floor. Depending on the size of the home, multiple detectors may be required on each floor. I know some may say test them once a month, I say once a week. It takes one minute out of your day. If a detector fails, contact your landlord as they must remedy the issue immediately. If they fail to do so, contact your local fire inspector's office. The fire department will send an inspector out quickly and contact your landlord issuing an order to comply, usually within twenty-four hours. The order also comes with a huge fine if they fail to comply. The fire inspector will leave you a copy of the order as well as their business card for any follow-up. Do not hesitate to call them back once the time limit on the order has expired if the issue was not rectified. As there are several types of smoke detectors on the market, its good to know what type is in your home.

Types include:

- Battery operated, batteries are replaceable.
- Hard wired (directly connected to the power in the home).
- 10-year models (battery cannot be replaced) the entire unit must be replaced.
- Dual Smoke and CO (Carbon Monoxide) 10-year model.

All types of detectors are great if they are installed correctly and the batteries are never removed. Local and city governments have and will mandate hardwired units as the law. I have been in many rental homes and have seen smoke detectors removed completely, detectors open with the batteries removed. In several instances, I saw plastic bags duct taped over the detectors. Simply put, Stupid. Stupid, Stupid. There is absolutely no reason to do this. You will forget to put the batteries back or reinstall the detector.

FIRE EXTINGUISHERS

Learn how a fire extinguisher works. It does not take long for a small fire to turn into an inferno. Remain calm, take the extinguisher in your hands, remove the pin, aim the nozzle at the base of the fire and squeeze the trigger. Use short controlled bursts until the fire is out. Never worry about the cleanup. Empty it out over the fire, as once the trigger is pulled the unit must be refilled or replaced. Make sure the fire is out. If you're unsure call 911 and ask for fire. Never feel embarrassed, fire is tricky and can hide inside walls and restart at any time. Remember, fire requires oxygen, therefore, it may burn unnoticed as it has a constant supply of it.

ABC Type fire extinguishers are the most commonly found in homes.

Ensure that you know where all units are mounted, the most common placement for extinguishers are the kitchen, main entrance foyer, and upper-level hallway.   If you are on the upper floor(s) and detect fire on the lower levels, take the fire extinguisher down with you as you may not be able to reach the fire extinguishers there.

Fire extinguishers located in the kitchen should never be placed near the oven or inside cabinets. They should be wall mounted as far away from the oven as possible as the most likely source of a kitchen fire in the oven itself. There is a dial on the extinguisher that indicates if it is fully charged. Also, fire extinguishers should be certified yearly. Check all the extinguishers for charge and take note of the certification dates that are written on the tag attached to the extinguisher.

Remember, never, ever pour water on a grease or oil fire. Stay calm, if you feel overwhelmed if the fire is growing, scream fire get out of the house to safety then call 911.

*Do not call from inside the house #dead

*Do not waste time looking for any personal belongings. #going shopping

Make sure you notify the landlord if you had to use it. The cost of recharging, certification and yearly inspection is the landlord's responsibility.

If you have been exposed to smoke from a fire call 911 and seek medical attention. Smoke inhalation can result in death.

CARBON MONOXIDE (CO) DETECTORS

These detectors measure the concentration of CO (Carbon Monoxide) in the home. CO is created when natural gas burns. If you have a forced air gas furnace supplying the heat in your home or an "On Demand" hot water system (usually gas operated) then as with smoke detectors, there must be a CO detector on every floor. CO is a silent killer. You cannot smell it, you cannot see or hear it. It will give you zero warning while you sleep. You simply never wake up. Equally, during your waking hours, you may feel drowsy and not realize you are slowly being poisoned until it is too late.

TYPES OF CARBON MONOXIDE (CO) DETECTORS INCLUDE:

- Plug in models with battery backup. Batteries are replaceable

- Hard wired (directly connected to the power in the home)

- 10-year models (battery cannot be replaced) the entire unit must be replaced

- Dual Smoke and CO (Carbon Monoxide)

Surprisingly, many CO detectors are improperly installed. The detectors work best by being installed higher up on a wall or in the case of dual smoke and CO detectors on the ceiling. When CO is introduced to a room it fills it "top-down" basically it starts at the ceiling and works its way down to the floor. Plug-in CO detectors are found in conventional power receptacles, far too low in the room. If your house has one improperly installed let your landlord know. They are responsible not only to provide the detectors but to properly install them.

SMOKING INDOORS

With the legalization of marijuana, more people are smoking inside their home. Between cigarettes and marijuana, the risk of fire is ever present. Eliminate this risk by simply smoking outdoors. Make sure that even outdoors you properly put out your smokables. Keep in mind that a landlord can charge you to repaint, clean, replace blinds or other window coverings that have been damaged by smoking indoors.

CHAPTER 6

PEST CONTROL & CLEANLINESS

Pest control is the responsibility of the landlord, but when it comes to those little bloodsucking bed bugs, you may be asked to pay part or all the expense for treatment. Ask your landlord and the current tenants if they ever had an issue with bed bugs or any other pest related problems.

MICE AND RATS

Rodents will get into your food, clothing and even inside a mattress. The most serious issue is they transmit, through urine, feces or bites the Hantavirus to humans, which can result in death. These are steps to take to help prevent and treat infestation:

- Keep floors, sinks, and counters clean.

- Use kitchen garbage can with lids.

- Place all garbage outside in sealed garbage bags. Keep garbage cans clean.

- Avoid placing food waste in bedroom garbage cans.

- Do not leave food in open containers (even in the cupboard or pantry) or in plates or bowels.

- If you identify access point outside the home, inform your landlord.

- If you see mouse droppings, spray with bleach (saturate) wait ten minutes, place droppings into a garbage bag and put bag in an outside garbage can. Spray and clean dustpan with bleach.

- Never sweep up or vacuum wet or dry droppings.

- Once a month pull out stove(s) and refrigerator(s) from walls and clean the area.

For more information on Hantavirus visit https://www.cdc.gov/hantavirus/hps/symptoms.html

RACOONS, SQUIRRELS, SKUNKS AND OPOSSUMS

In one of our student homes, we found all four of these critters cohabitating. They had dug access holes in the backyard and were living in the crawl-space basement. The students were leaving garbage bags outside of the home in the rear and at the side so food was only a short walk away. The cost to evict these animals was about twenty-five hundred dollars.

Here are tips to help prevent a zoo:

- If you hear or see any of these critters in or around your home contact the landlord immediately.
- Never feed them. There cute, yes, until there using the inside of your home as a toilet.

- They could have rabies.

- They carry parasites, fleas, and even ticks.

- Keep all garbage secured in bins with lids. The landlord is responsible for providing bins.

- Keep barbeques clean, including the little grease tray at the bottom.

We all love our pets, but I would strongly recommend that during your time off campus that you avoid introducing pets in your home.

COCKROACHES

Once you develop a cockroach problem it takes several treatments to exterminate them. Proper treatment requires a lot of preparation and cleaning on your part such as:

- Empty all your kitchen cupboards, your pantry, the top, and bottom cupboards.

- Pull the refrigerator(s), stove(s) away from the wall.

- Clear the countertops.

- Empty out your closets.

- Dressers, side tables, and beds must be pulled away from the wall.

- All the floors, countertops and cupboards must be cleaned.

Once the first treatment is complete, a common mistake is cleaning the cupboards, countertops and washing the floors next to the baseboards. Doing this negates the treatment. Basically, you're washing away the treatment agents so leave these areas alone for a few weeks.

BED BUGS

As far as I'm concerned, the worst critters to deal with are bed bugs. Bedbugs are transported. They are not a result of poor hygiene or cleanliness. Five-star hotels have them. A friend can bring them into your home. Here are some tips for you to help minimize the chances of being infested:

- Talk about it. The negative stigma associated with bed bugs helps spread them. There is no need to be embarrassed. Warn your guests that you have or had them. Ask them if they have had issues.

- Ask every guest if they have recently stayed in a motel, even for one night. If possible, place their clothing in the dryer for fifteen minutes on high.

- Check your lease for the bed bug clause. You may be responsible to pay for treatment. Treatments can cost thousands of dollars.

- Never buy a used mattress.

- Avoid bringing furniture home you found left curbside.

- Once a week when you change and wash your bed sheets and pillowcases (yes, I said once a week) inspect your mattress and box spring.

Traveling?

If you plan to stay at a motel/hotel before you unpack, do the following:

1. Leave your bags/luggage outside in the car or hallway.
2. Go to your room and lift the bedding, using a flashlight (your phone) inspect the entire perimeter of the mattress. Check the mattress seams, as they will lay

eggs and generally congregate there, close to their food (you!)

3. Lift the mattress and inspect the box spring.

4. Inspect along the headboard (in a motel its usually attached to the wall) use the flashlight to check the gap between the headboard and wall.

5. Inspect around the wall mounted pictures as well.

6. Once the room has passed inspection: enjoy your stay. If you are worried about bringing them home, travel with a few large clear garbage bags. Put all your clothing in the bags. When you arrive home to place your clothing in the dryer on high for fifteen minutes.

THE HOUSE CENTIPEDE

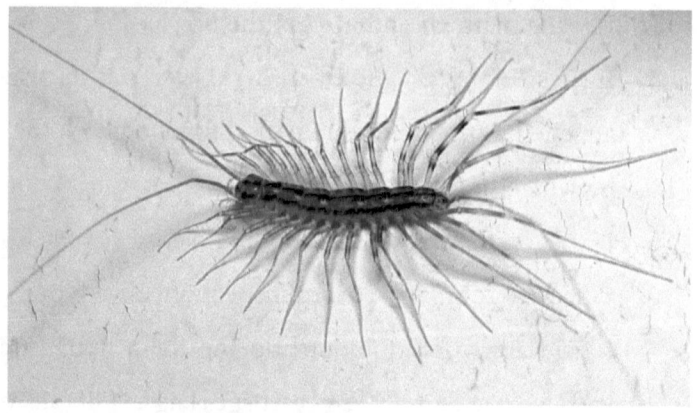

Believe it or not, these little critters are your live-in pest control agents. I know your first impulse is to smoosh it. DON'T! I sat on the telephone with a student whose trembly voice described this multi-legged creature skirting across her bed. She was terrified. The way the poor girl was going on you would think this thing could give Godzilla a hard time. I explained how these insects kill spiders, cockroaches, flies and bed bugs. If you see them, odds are you have one or all their prey somewhere in your home. Cool fact, when the centipede feels threatened it will detach a leg or two to keep a predator off its tail so it can escape. The house centipede likes it dark and damp. The only downside here is its sting is like a bees. Believe me, they are more terrified of you, if you can get past their creepy exterior and let them be, they will help you exterminate many other creepy crawlies.

CLEANLINESS

"Clean your room!" You have been hearing that as far back as you can remember. Words of wisdom. All manner of creepy crawlies love your messes, especially food waste. Mice, rats, spiders, ants, and cockroaches will crawl all over you to eat the yummies you have on your bed.

White vinegar is a great (and cheap) cleaning agent. Both full strength and diluted with warm water. Vinegar can repel ants and spiders. You can use it to trap fruit flies. There are literally over a hundred uses for white vinegar.

- Mop your floors and clean all household surfaces with vinegar and warm water. It not only cleans those surfaces but disinfects them. Yes, the smell is a little funky but the benefits out the way it.

- Mix vinegar with baking soda to unclog sinks and disinfect them.

- Run vinegar through your coffee maker or kettle.

- Place ½ cup vinegar and ½ cup water into a bowl, place the bowl in the microwave and press start until it boils, then wipe clean.

- Spray vinegar onto cutting boards scrub then rinse.

- Use one cup in your laundry as a replacement for fabric softener.

- Make 50/50 water and vinegar mix as a general disinfectant for surfaces like faucets, telephones, doorknobs.

Viruses are becoming more and more resistant to treatment. Wash your hands frequently and properly.

CHAPTER 7
WATER DAMAGE & MANAGEMENT

Every year billions of dollars in property damage is caused by burst water pipes. During the winter months, the risk is significantly greater. The main water line is comprised of a meter and shut off valve. Turning off this main valve will stop the flow of water into your home. Generally, this main valve is in the basement level against an exterior wall closest to the street. If you cannot find it yourself or are unsure, ask your landlord to advise you of its location. See figure 1.

Figure 1

Water pipes can burst any time of year and the possibility exist that the furnace, boiler or electrical heaters can fail. If the heat source in the home fails and the outside temperature is low enough, water pipes can freeze rapidly. You're going to find that in many of the older homes, water pipes are not properly insulated, there's a lot of exposed piping and this can contribute to pipes freezing. If your house will be empty during school breaks, it's a good idea to shut off the main water supply valve and to turn on a tap in the lowest point of the house in order to release all the water in the lines. This will help prevent any type of damage from frozen pipes while you are away. Another preventative measure during extreme cold conditions is to turn on the water taps to allow a fine stream to run. Moving water will not freeze. Although wasteful, as a freeze prevention method it's worth the extra expense. Although you may be thinking these are measures the landlord should be responsible for, I believe it's a perfect opportunity to learn and understand the inner workings of a house, not only for the prevention of a disaster for yourself as a future homeowner.

Remember your belongings may be damaged. It's recommended when you go out on winter break that you leave the thermostat set at its original setting, never turn it down or off.

A group of students was renting on a "utilities included" basis. Thinking they were doing the landlord a favor, one of the students turned off the heat before they went on winter break. Instead of saving money, it cost the landlord ten-thousand dollars. Turning down the heat caused the pipes to freeze and turning the heat back on caused them to burst. In a similar case, damages amounted to thirty-thousand dollars. In both cases, the landlords did not have insurance to cover the damages and the students paid for the damages, well, their parents did.

TOILETS

You may find a clause in your lease that states that you are responsible for clogged toilets or drain lines. The cost for these types of repairs can be very expensive. The average cost to unplug or "snake" a toilet is one-hundred dollars. More serious issues can involve the removal of toilets and the need for a "Water-Jetti" (a high-pressure water line and camera that clears clogged pipes). These types of services can cost thousands.

To avoid these costs, keep the following items out of the toilet:

- Sanitary products

- Wipes (even if it says flushable on the package).

- Cigarette butts.

- Hair (hair will build up and cause blockages).

- Medications: Prescriptions or otherwise.

- Chemicals opt for environmentally friendly alternatives. (vinegar)

There are only three things that belong in the toilet:

1. Pee
2. Poo
3. Toilet paper

Leaking or running toilets can cause a utility bill to skyrocket. I have personally seen water bills that were twenty times normal. In this case, two toilets in the home were constantly running and the tenants simply ignored it. When you notice your toilet running or leaking, inform the landlord immediately. A leaking toilet can cause damage to walls, floors, and ceilings.

North Americans are blessed with clean running water, showers and indoor toilets. So blessed that often we forget and take it for granted. We leave the water running while we brush our teeth. We turn on the shower and let it run until we are ready to go in. We stand away from the water stream in the shower while we lather, wash and condition our hair. We fill our bathtubs with enough water for four people to shower. We flush and flush millions of gallons of potable water literally down the toilet. Funny thing is that most of the planet does not share in our fortune. If you consider the people that literally must walk one day's journey just to arrive at a water well and carry back the water another day to their families. They do this over and over with no assurance of how safe that water is to drink. Statistically worldwide nearly only 20% of wastewater enters the ecosystem treated.

- 340,000 children under five die every year from diarrheal diseases that otherwise are preventable if clean water and proper sanitation were available.

- Almost 2.5 billion people have zero access to the basics of sanitation.

- Nearly 4.5 billion do not have a toilet in their homes.

I have heard many people say, "We pay for and should be able to enjoy these luxuries". I can assure you that one day the cost of water will be astronomical. Water has already become a scarce commodity around the world. Consider our planet and help preserve as much as you can.

CHAPTER 8

ELECTRICAL SAFETY

Be alert when dealing with electricity, if you're not sure to ASK!!! Many homes around campus are older and although they might have been renovated in some way, generally those renovations are done as inexpensively as possible which may mean older wiring, outlets, switches, and panels. What you need to know from day one is where the circuit breaker panel located. Usually it's found in the basement of the home. You might have a two-breaker split, this means that you'll find one on the main level or an upper level. This is because there was new wiring installed and basically they ran the main line down to the main panel and bridged off of that which allows you not to have to go down to the basement if lights go off on the second floor or third floor. Find the location of the main panel. See figure 2

Figure 2

Stay away from electrical panels as seen in figure 3.

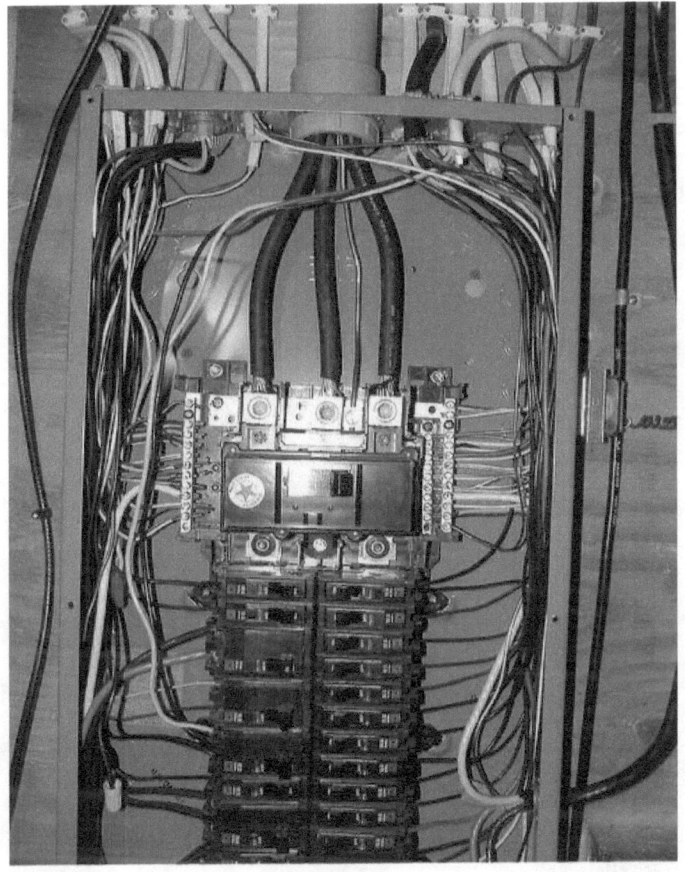

Figure 3

In an ideal situation, the circuit breakers are labeled. I have seen lease inclusions that say specifically if you trip a circuit breaker because you overloaded it (by plugging in too many appliances in one outlet) the fees vary from twenty-five to one-hundred dollars to have someone come and reset the circuit breaker(s). Some landlords charge seventy-five dollars to change a light bulb.

Warning!!! Before you touch the breaker panel, even the exterior cover, make sure the area around the panel is well lit, otherwise use a flashlight and look down on the ground to make sure that you're not standing in water. Do not touch a circuit breaker if it seems loose or is visibly broken. Contact the landlord.

As a group, get together and buy a four- or five-foot step ladder. Never climb up on tables or chairs to change out bulbs. I recommend asking the landlord to remove any compact fluorescent bulb located in the home. See figure 4

Figure 4

CFL bulbs contain mercury. The EPA has a four-page guide for proper cleanup and disposal of broken CFL bulbs. I have included a link. https://www.epa.gov/cfl/cleaning-broken-cfl Keep a box of spare lights in the house. And if the landlord does not provide extra bulbs, buy them.

CHAPTER 9
RENTAL AND SECURITY DEPOSITS

Ontario Canada has one of North Americas strictest rental laws. In Ontario the following deposits are not permitted;

- Security.
- Damage.
- Pet.
- Key (*an actual deposit for the replacement cost of a key is permitted but not for locks or the costs to replace them*) This usually the case in condominiums.

Permitted deposits:

- First and Last month's rent.
- Replacement key deposit.

In North America, most regions have similar rules in place relating to rental deposits. Across the country pet deposits are permitted and average four-hundred dollars, except Ontario and service animals are generally exempt. Many landlords will ask for multiple deposits even though they are not legal in that jurisdiction. It is up to you to perform due diligence and confirm local laws or simply accept the terms. Landlords are not asking for these deposits out of greed, the reality is it's very difficult to collect money for damages after you have moved out.

CHAPTER 10

SUBLETTING

All landlords prefer full twelve-month lease terms for students. The ideal scenario is an eight-month lease, you will find that you may lose that perfect home if you are firm on eight months. Some landlords will permit you to sub-lease for the four-month term, but you are generally responsible for arranging it. The landlord may even ask to approve the sub-letters as well. This means you may still be responsible for the rent. As a sub-letter, be careful and ensure you have a document from the landlord that approves the sublet. Otherwise, you may find yourself being evicted.

Here are some of the problems you may face:

- Damages that may occur are your responsibility.
- Difficulty finding students to sublet may equate to you having to subsidize a portion of the rent.
- Students have reported thefts from their rooms. Although it's not your fault, it may cause tensions between you and your roommates.
- You may have difficulty getting the sublease student out of the room if they have difficulty finding accommodations.

- Proper vetting (verification of references) of subletting student usually does not occur. This may result in renting rooms to non-students, which has security implications. Surprisingly over the years, I have had several non-students, including men in their forties and fifties (creepers!), try to rent in student homes.

CHAPTER 11

SAFETY AND SECURITY

We take our safety and security for granted. We never truly expect to be victims, and this means we let our guard down. I am not telling you to be paranoid or live in fear, just be conscientious.

Two years ago, I received a telephone call from a female student at 1:00 pm. Her home was located directly on a corner of a very busy main road. You could easily see the entire property from the road. She informed me that someone had broken into the home. The rear entrance door to the home was badly damaged and she went on to say the bedroom doors had been smashed in so badly that they had been split in two. Furthermore, it was obvious that laptops were missing along with other electronics. At that point, I realized she was walking through the home describing the mayhem. I asked if her roommates were with her. She told me she was alone. I immediately told her to get out, cross the street and call 911, and call me back.

I could not believe she had entered the home alone. I explained to her that whoever had broken in may still be there. They were brazened enough to violently enter during the day, who knows if they were aware of the girl's class schedules. The most troubling part was she was about to go upstairs to check the rooms.

When we spoke again, I explained that I am not the first person you call and even if there are all five girls present (hold on, I am not saying that the ladies cannot handle themselves, put down the cell phones) what I am saying is, male students are rarely the targets of sexual assault. Simply because you have not heard about it on campus does not mean it has not or does not happen.

Just because you know martial arts or think you can take on the world (hey, been there, done that) In the real world, knives and bullets kill, you do not get "extra lives" you cannot see behind you and when confronted you do not know how many there are. Your best defense whenever possible: Run!

Here are a few tips to improve your safety:

- Trust your gut, instinct is a powerful weapon. If something or someone seems off, they most likely are.

- Make sure your home has exterior lighting (sensor activated) over each door. If the lights are not automatic and you have control of the switch from the inside leave it on twenty-four seven. Never approach the rear of the home or a front porch that is blocked by trees, shrubs or any design that obstructs the view from the street.

- Never assume. If there is a stranger at the door, any door, call out to them from the sidewalk or the end of the driveway and ask if you may help them. Do not feel embarrassed. If they need a signature for a package, then sign it in plain sight out in the open. Aside from the landlord, never allow anyone to inspect the interior of the home. Never permit utility resellers to enter the house, even if they have those official ID badges.

- If you are using any social media platforms including Craigslist or Kijiji to buy and sell, always meet in a public area. Avoid inviting anyone to your house.

- If you see a suspicious vehicle parked in your area, note the license plate number and contact the police directly, not 911.

- Note campus security stations, emergency call locations.

- Always be aware of your surroundings.

- During evening hours pair up. Avoid walking alone at night.

- When my daughter attended the University of Toronto, I gave her this tip: never park your car next to a van and if you are returning to your car and there is a van parked next to you, go back and wait, or have someone escort you from campus security. From the day you start driving use this tip.

- Never leave handbags, wallets, laptops, phones, backpacks, or bags visible in your car.

- Back up data frequently in the event of theft or loss of your electronics.

- Never leave spare house keys hidden around the outside of your home. Criminals shop too, so they know all about the fake rock hide a key.

- Never make key copies for friends or partners. If you have electronic locks, never give that code out.

- If you decide to meet people over dating or hook up apps, let your roommates know where, who, and when. If you're getting picked up, snap a pic of the license plate and send it to a friend. Hey, no judgment, just be safe.

Quick fact:

The cost of the components necessary to obtain your financial information from public Wi-Fi is about eighty dollars. Avoid banking or purchasing online utilizing free or open Wi-Fi sources.

CHAPTER 12
YOUR CAR AND PARKING

If you are fortunate enough to have your own vehicle, consider the following:

- While house hunting confirm you have a parking space. Never assume you do just because there is a driveway. If your renting as a single student, be sure to ask, as students tend to rent out parking spots, especially business or economics majors.

- In most cases be prepared to play driveway Tetris. Older homes have short driveways or share a driveway with the adjoining house. This means you will probably be moving your car around to accommodate other students.

- Landlords may say "there is plenty of street parking" but you may find yourself ticketed or towed as there may be a lack of overnight street parking. If a landlord advises you parking is available at the home, ensure it is in your lease.

- Never leave backpacks, laptops, purses or wallets in your vehicle. "smash and grab" thefts occur on campus, your driveway, public parking any time of the day.

CHAPTER 13

YOUR LEASE

Leases come in all shapes and sizes. Landlords try to include as many "rules" as possible. In many cases, inclusions in your lease contravene the landlord and tenant act. This does not simply negate the lease itself. Those inclusions are simply unenforceable. Landlords rarely seek an audience with the courts for several reasons. The main reason is their property violates building codes. Now, this is important: It's not a reason to take advantage of a landlord. Although this guide is for your protection, I remind you that causing financial harm to a landlord, in the end, results in higher costs to the students. It has led to students being forced to vacate the home by order of the building department.

I have no pity for slumlords, they, as I said before, are fair game, but just because a landlord has unlawful inclusions in their lease by no means qualifies them as a slumlord. We all at times try to establish ground rules that we hope everyone will agree to and follow. All good landlords want is their properties kept clean, (remember the pest control chapter) and damage free, and of course the rent on time. Remember that civility is a two-way street. There are rules and when you decide to move out it is expected that you will follow the rules as the landlord is expected to do so.

I had spoken about trying to find a home that you could live in for your entire school term. The landlord and tenant act require that you give sixty days' notice if you intend to move. This means that between 8:00 am and 8:00 pm the landlord can show your home to prospective students. The number one complaint from students is regarding showings. Personal items go missing, floors and carpeting get dirty, students go through the home unescorted. If the showings go on too long, it can become very tedious. Usually the further from campus your home is the longer it takes to rent.

A FINAL THOUGHT

There are certain choices we make in our lives that will significantly influence our future. I never was one to sugar coat anything. I can tell you that you cannot erase your past, only that you can change in the future who you were in the past. I can also tell you that photograph or video recording of you doing anything stupid, will be available for everyone to see, forever. This includes graduate school admissions, the professor your about to hand your dissertation to, future employers and even a future partner. We all can now easily search to see exactly how stupid you can be. Today, life is as public as a majestic tree in a park. If you are a violent idiot when you consume alcohol, then don't consume alcohol. If you have a problem with alcohol, drugs or violence, there are meetings every day to help you. Meetings on or off campus.

Pressures in school can seem so overwhelming that we do certain things to drown that pain out. By the time we realize we have crossed that line, stepping back seems impossible. It's not. Every one of you has made this effort to improve your lives to guarantee a better future. There are many people out there, including your teachers, that want you to succeed and are willing to help you do it.

Ask anyone over forty if they would like to trade places with you. Betcha we all say yes!

Never be embarrassed to ask for help. People may judge, their comments or opinions simply do not matter. There will always be people out there that thrive on the misery of others. As you get older you will easily identify them and exclude them from your inner circle.

Identifying a weakness in yourself and asking for help is the bravest step you could ever take.

Obstacles placed before you are not worth your life. Unfortunately, we all lose people we love; friends and family may become ill, careers are lost and relationships end. We may fail exams and even courses. These are side effects of life. We need connections with each other. Once one is severed, there are more to help us cope. I believe that is how we are wired. A single individual will not have all the answers, together we do.

THE END

RENT AND SECURITY DEPOSITS BY STATE & PROVINCE

Alabama	**1 month's rent.**
Alaska	2 month's rent.
Alberta	1 months' rent.
Arizona	1-1/2 months' rent.
Arkansas	2 months' rent.
British Columbia	½ of 1 months' rent
California	2 months'
Colorado	Unlimited
Connecticut	2 months' rent
Delaware	2 month's rent
District of Columbia	1 month's rent.
Florida	Unlimited.
Georgia	Unlimited.
Hawaii	1 month rent.
Idaho	Unlimited.
Illinois Unlimited.	Unlimited.
Indiana	Unlimited.
Iowa	2 months' rent.
Kansas	1 month rent.
Kentucky	Unlimited.

Louisiana	Unlimited.
Maine	2 months' rent.
Manitoba	½ months' rent
Maryland	2 months' rent.
Massachusetts	1 month rent.
Michigan	1-1/2 month's rent.
Minnesota	Unlimited.
Mississippi	Unlimited.
Missouri	2 months' rent.
Montana	Unlimited.
Nebraska	1 month rent
Nevada	3 months' rent
New Brunswick	1 months' rent
Newfoundland & Labrador.	75% of 1 months' rent.
New Hampshire	1 month rent
New Jersey	1-1/2 month's rent.
New Mexico	Unlimited.
New York	Unlimited.
North Carolina	2 months' rent
North Dakota	$1500.00 maximum
Nova Scotia	½ months" rent.
Nunavut	1 months' rent.
Ohio	Unlimited.
Oklahoma	Unlimited.
Ontario	2 Months
Oregon	Unlimited.

P.E.I.	1 months' rent
Pennsylvania	2 months' rent.
Rhode Island	1 months' rent.
Quebeczero	(first months' rent only)
Saskatchewan	1 months' rent.
South Carolina	Unlimited.
South Dakota	1 month rent.
Tennessee	Unlimited.
Texas	Unlimited.
Utah	Unlimited.
Vermont	Unlimited.
Virginia	2 months' rent.
Washington	Unlimited.
West Virginia	Unlimited.
Wisconsin	Unlimited.
Wyoming	Unlimited.

TOP 50 US CITIES FOR BED BUGS

1. Baltimore
2. Washington, D.C.
3. Chicago
4. Los Angeles
5. Columbus, Ohio
6. New York
7. Cincinnati
8. Detroit
9. Atlanta
10. Philadelphia
11. Cleveland-Akron
12. San Francisco
13. Raleigh-Durham, N.C.
14. Indianapolis
15. Dallas
16. Norfolk, Va.
17. Richmond, Va.
18. Greenville, S.C.
19. Charlotte, N.C.
20. Grand Rapids, Mich.
21. Buffalo, N.Y.
22. Knoxville, Tenn.

23. Nashville, Tenn.

24. Champaign,

25. Pittsburgh

26. Houston

27. Denver

28. Milwaukee

29. Miami

30. Louis

31. Charleston, W.Va.

32. Lansing, Mich.

33. Syracuse, N.Y.

34. Phoenix

35. Tampa, Fla.

36. Greensboro, N.C.

37. Omaha, Neb.

38. Boston

39. Seattle

40. Las Vegas

41. Orlando, Fla.

42. Davenport43. Hartford, Conn.

43. Cedar Rapids, Iowa

44. Dayton, Ohio

45. Honolulu

46. Flint, Mich.

47. Wayne, Ind.

48. San Diego

49. Youngstown, Ohio

TOP 10 CANADIAN CITIES FOR BED BUGS

1.   Toronto
2.   Winnipeg
3.   St. John's
4.   Vancouver
5.   Halifax
6.   Ottawa
7.   Hamilton
8.   Sudbury
9.   Windsor
1.   10.Scarborough

Acknowledgements

Edited By Cinzia Macri

Liv Weller

Sara - Leadingtranscriptions.com

UNITED NATIONS, UNESCO, WHO

Itamar Croitoru-Open Door Windows and Doors Inc.

Escape windows

www.ingramcontent.com/pod-product-compliance
Lightning Source LLC
Chambersburg PA
CBHW031257280526
45784CB00004B/1886